The Man With A Hammer by Anna Wickham

Anna Wickham was the main pseudonym used by Edith Alice Mary Harper who was born on 7th May 1883, Wimbledon, Surrey.

Her first poetry collection was published privately in 1911 under another pseudonym, John Oland. Appropriately enough it was called Songs by John Oland. The main theme of the book was the difficulties of relationships between men and women. Unfortunately, her possessive husband was very upset at her publication, having also shown little support for her earlier singing and acting careers. It led to violent quarrels and sadly Anna had a nervous breakdown and was admitted to a private psychiatric hospital for a period of six weeks.

Shortly after recovering, she met Harold Monro at his Poetry Bookshop. He encouraged her writing, and this led to a second collection being published in 1915. Her life now became increasingly split between domesticity and the yearned for bohemian life that was now calling her.

Whilst the poetry volumes she released are small in number she left behind several hundred unpublished poems that survived both the war and her life. Today she is regarded as a leading Modernist poet who was able to frankly express her desires and feelings through verse despite these often being at odds with the prevailing morals of the day.

Index of Contents

The Shrew
Reward
The Sad Lover
The Artificer
Necromancy
The Recompense
Flagellant
The Stormy Moon
Words
Abdication
Aseptic
Divorce
Nervous Prostration
The Fired Pot
Retrospect
The Pioneer
Traducers
The Choice
The Promise
The Assignation
Ceremony
Service
The Cruel Lover
Remembrance
State Endowment
Ordeal
The Faithful Mother
After Annunciation
A Boy's Mouth
The Mother-in-Law
The Individualist
The Walk
All Men to Women
A Girl in Summer
The Anchorite
The Song-maker
Imperatrix
Song of Anastasia
Question
The Conscience
Song of the Weak
Release
The Contrast
Tatterdemalion
The Ghost
Women and Multitudes
The Woman's Mind
Self-esteem
The Avenue
The Solace
Warning

THE MAN WITH A HAMMER

My Dear was a mason
And I was his stone.
And quick did he fashion
A house of his own.

As fish in the waters,

As birds in a tree,
So natural and blithe lives
His spirit in me.

INVITATION

Come, my Content,
The hungry days are spent!—
Beauty, illumine me
As sunlight fills a narrow waveless sea!

EXAMINATION

If my work is to be good,
I must transcend skill, I must master mood.
For the expression of the rare thing in me.
Is not in do, but deeper, in to be.
Something of this kind was meant,
When piety was likened to a scent.
A smell is not in movement, not in power,
It is a function of a perfect flower.

I only compass something rare,
By the high form of willing which is prayer.
A ship transcendent and a sword of fire.
For me, the traveller, is in desire.
I write my thought in this most ragged way.
That being baulked of beauty, I am stung to pray.

RETURN OF PLEASURE

I thought there was no pleasure in the world
Because of my fears.
Then I remembered life and all the words in my language.
And I had courage even to despise form.
I thought, "I have skill to make words dance.
To clap hands and to shake feet.
But I will put myself, and everything I see, upon the page.
Why should I reject words because of their genealogy?
Or things, because of their association."
Why should I scorn a bus rather than a ship?"

FECUNDITY

Fret and strain.
And ugly signs of pain,
Never yet had part
In birth of Art.
Men are brought forth in grief,
Labour for Beauty is a soul's relief.
Expression is conceived, and has its shape,
Of Sloth's most painful violent rape.
A spirit big with Beauty shall be discontent,
She knows all rapture when her time is spent.
Go! my sick striving spirit, seek
A simple, swift, victorious technique!

RESOLUTION

I will not draw only a house or a tree,
I will draw very Me;
Everything I think, everything I see!

I will have no shame,
No hope of praise or fear of blame!
These things are mean things, and the same.

I am the product of old laws,
Old effect of old cause.
The thing that is, may make the blind gods pause.

FORMALIST

As men whose bones are wind-blown dust, have sung,
Let me sing now!
I'll sing of gourds, and goads, of honey, and the plough.
I am a raw uneasy parvenu,
I am uncertain of my time.
How can I pour the liquor of new days
In the old pipes of Rhyme."

COMMENT

Tone
Is utterly my own.
Far less exterior than skill.
It comes from the deep centre of the will;
For nobler qualities of Song,

Not singing, but the singer must be strong.

NOTE ON RHYME

Likeness of sound,
With just enough of difference
To make a change of sense;
So we have contrast,
A piquancy,
And a certain victory of contrivance.
But Heaven keep us from an inevitable rhyme,
Or from a rhyme prepared!
Rhymed verse is a wide net
Through which many subtleties escape.
Nor would I take it to capture a strong thing,
Such as a whale.

THE POET IN THE HOUSE

A small oak grew in an elder-hedge.
Rustling with growth, he said,
"I am an oak, an oak!"
The elders bent to him with heavy scent.
Taunting, "O, little weed!"

The oak shrank into himself, and made ready to die.
But a wave of courage swept over him
Deep from the heart of his mother-oak.
He drew himself up with passion, crying still,
"I am an oak."

He pressed himself against the coward leaves.
Up against the heavy scent.
And he prevailed!
In future days, there will be no elder-hedge,
Only an oak.

FEAR OF THE SUPREME

I dreamed that I was hungry all day long,
Until at night I ate a song.
It was as if I dined upon the Host, and so was satisfied;
But of ecstatic surfeit quick I died.

O! Love, come to me now, and hold me fast,

Lest I should eat that deadly food at last.

A WOMAN IN BED

Sometimes when I go to rest
I lie and struggle for expression,
And failing, fall to sick depression.
And beat my breast.

By blows, I cannot 'scape
The utter irritation
Of my poor soul's frustration,
For so I know my shape.

And often have I found
An added sadness.
Bringing me to madness,
Because my breast is round.

How can I, being woman,
Dedicate nights
Which should be sacred to delights,
To this lust of words, which is so broadly human

But through the well-clothed days
I can forget my skirt,
I hide my breast beneath a workman's shirt.
And hunt the perfect phrase.

THE RECLUSE

I'm tired of living in the town,
Of trailing up, and trailing down.
My very heart feels like a street,
Sullied with busy living and with dusty feet.

Nor is there any peace for me in fields,
There I remember crops and market-yields.
In the quiet cow I have no gain,
For she recalls loud milk-cans on a train.

I dream that there is harbourage for me.
In the blue breath of some remoter sea.
On a brown rock weed-tipt to malachite,
Where sea-gulls wheeling from their track, alight.

There I would live, with gulls'-eggs for my food.

My only recreation, to be good,
With only passing Time for fate,
Free of my friends, and cool without a mate.

Give me an hour
Of perfect freedom and of power!—
When I see done
All things I longed for 'neath the Sun—
Then let me die
A flame-burst to the Sky!

O my Lover blind me,
Take your cords and bind me,
Then drive me through a silent land,
With the compelling of your open hand!

There is too much of sound, too much for sight.
In thunderous lightnings of this night,
There is too much of freedom for my feet,
Bruised by the stones of this disordered street.

I know that there is sweetest rest for me.
In silent fields, and in captivity.
O Lover! drive me through a stilly land,
With the compelling of your open hand.

I am so tired I cannot move,
I would sit still and love.
I carried souls so long in pain,
I too would be a child again.

Man who is not child to woman
Is either rogue or more than human.—
I rested once upon my father's strength:
O to find peace in love at length!

Man, are you strong to take my proffered hand.
And to be kind when you command.''
There was a saint who carried children up a steep,

Make me your child, and let me sleep.

I have no rest,
I am a guest at best,
I can be driven from the house,
Like bat or mouse,
If I please not the house's lord.
For bed and board.

I spend my days
In dull sequestered ways.
Without right to praise.
My brain dies
For want of exercise,
I dare not speak.
For I am weak.

'Twere better for my man and me,
If I were free.
Not to be done by, but to be.
But I am tied.
Free movement is denied.
I am a man's wife,
For all my life!

My enemy!
If you would work the ruin of my mind,
You must not hit me with this ignominy.
You must be kind.

I am soothed and drugged by kindness,
Till I sleep,
But I find a tongue in blindness
When I weep!

This is too rare a festival for joy,
As was that joy too rare for my worn kisses,
When first I put a babe to my good breast.
Then was my body justified, with love.

And all such enterprise.

When I conceived that good plan
I made no feudal compact with my man,
For in my body's service is not found
A warrant that my will be always bound.

Now, being mother, this I see
I am thrice woman, and the soul of me
Is herded to an end I never sought
Like cow or sheep, and my desire is naught.

Who can my fuller need divine.
From the curved symbol of my body's line?
So for a simple accident of shape.
To work all ruin with my soul's rape.

This is too rare a festival for joy,
For a new thing is born of other labours.
I will break an heirloom, shout and stamp for this new victory.
I will fling my freedom at the stars,
And with a good conceit think so to shake the spheres.
And when shall Heaven tremble.
But when tired eyes.
Scanning long empty spaces.
So see God.

OUTLINE

Man I shall beget to-morrow.
Where is he?
Life a load, the load a sorrow,
Better not to be.
Man I shall beget to-morrow.
Non-existent? Where is he?

He is spread in fields of wheat,
Low in grass that cows shall eat.
There are fragments of himself
High upon some warehouse shelf.
Any atom he may be.
Any atom may be he.

She the focus will control,
The new body, but the soul?"
That is free.
The husk is made of any meat.
Any grass or any wheat.
But man has personality;

He alone is he.
The man is- I get to-morrow
Whole in destiny.

Can I then be free?

DEFINITION

What is a wife?
Is it she who stays in a man's house for all her life?—
If wife were nothing more than that
Then she were equalled by a homing cat.

What is a wife? Shall it be said
She who by contract shares a bed?—
Go find a thousand wives complete
In girls that flaunt along the street!

Nor is it she, content with sequence from a cause,
Who, like a field increases by just laws.
And from a habit and with no end clear,
Brings forth a child for every wedded year.

Wives are the dreaming mothers come again
Who of blest fertile love bear souls of men!
Sometimes, with decorous silence, sometimes with stinging speech
Put a man's high attainment well within his reach.

There is a Virgin-Mother, shrined in Christianity,
There is a virgin wife in faiths to be.
For the constructive form-inducing principle for life.
Is she unknown, unnamed God's wife.
Who out of crystal bearing water drew the higher ape:—
She might give even Socialism a shape!

THE ANGRY WOMAN

I am a woman, with a woman's parts.
And of love I bear children.
In the days of bearing is my body weak,
But why because I do you service, should you call me slave?

I am a woman in my speech and gait,
I have no beard, (I'll take no blame for that!)
In many things are you and I apart,
But there are regions where we coincide,
Where law for one is law for both.

There is the sexless part of me that is my mind.
You calculate the distance of a star,
I, thanks to this free age can count as well.
And by the very processes you use.
When we think differently of two times two,
I'll own a universal mastery in you I—

Now of marriage,—
In marriage there are many mansions,
(This has been said of Heaven).
Shall you rule all the houses of your choice
Because of manhood or because of strength?
If I must own your manhood synonym for every strength.
Then must I lie.
If sex is a criterion for power, and never strength,
What do we gain by union?
I lose all, while nothing worthy is so gained by you,
O most blessed bond!

Because of marriage, I have motherhood.
That is much, and yet not all!

By the same miracle that makes me mother
Are you a father.

It is a double honour!
Are you content to be from henceforth only father,
And in no other way a man?
A fantastic creature like a thing of dreams
That has so great an eye it has no head.
I am not mother to abstract Childhood, but to my son,
And how can I serve my son, but to be much myself.

My motherhood must boast some qualities,
For as motherhood is diverse
So shall men be many charactered
And show variety, as this world needs.

Shall I for ever brush my infant's hair?"
Cumber his body in conceited needle-work?
Or shall I save some pains till he is grown?
Show him the consolation of mathematics
And let him laugh with me when I am old?"

If he is my true son.
He will find more joy in number and in laughter
Than in all these other things.

Why should dull custom make my son my enemy
So that the privilege of his manhood is to leave my house?

You would hold knowledge from me because I am a mother,
Rather for this reason let me be wise, and very strong,—
Power should be added to power.—

And now of love!—
There are many loves.

There is love, which is physiology,
And love, which has no more matter in it than is in the mind.
There is spiritual love, and there is good affection.
All these loves women need, and most of all the last.

Kiss me sometimes in the light,
Women have body's pain of body's love.
Let me have flowers sometimes, and always joy.
And sometimes let me take your hand and kiss you honestly
Losing nothing in dignity by frank love.
If I must fly in love and follow in life,
Doing both things falsely.
Then am I a mime,
I have no free soul.

Man! For your sake and for mine, and for the sake of future men.
Let me speak my mind in life and love.
Be strong for love of a strong mate.
Do not ask my weakness as a sacrifice to power.
When you deny me justice
I feel as if my body were in grip of a cold octopus.
While my heart is crushed to stone.

This rapture have I of pretence!

SONG OF THE LOW-CASTE WIFE

What have you given me for my strong sons?
O scion of kings!
In new veins the blood of old kings runs cold.
Your people thinking of old victories^ lose the lust of conquest.
Your men guard what they have,
Your women nurse their silver pots.
Dead beauty mocks hot blood!
What shall these women conceive of their chill loves
But still more pots?

But I have conceived of you new men;
Boys brave from the breast.
Running and striving like no children of your House,
And with their brave new brains
Making new myths.

My people were without, while yours were kings.
They sang the song of exile in low places
And in the stress of growth knew pain.
The unprepared world pressed hard upon them.
Women bent beneath burdens, while cold struck babes,
But they arose strong from the fight.
Hungry from their oppression.

And I am full of lust,
Which is not stayed with your old glories.
Give me for all old things that greatest glory—
A little growth.

Am I your mate because I share your bed?
Go then! Find each day a new mate outside your house.

I am your mate if I can share your vision.
Have you no vision, king-descended?
Come share mine!
Will you give me this, for your sons?
O scion of kings?

TO THE SILENT MAN

That you should love is not enough for me.
Come tell your love with pleasing courtesy.
I keep no faith in silence, I am wild and weak;
Now by the beauty of all wandering fires, I beg you speak.
Here is a rout of whispered loves and laughter,
And I must turn about and follow after.

To hymn Love, to live because of Beauty,
That is Love's life, that is a lover's duty,
Can you not see I weep because I go,
Speak, dumb Man! speak! Say, shall I stay or no?

SUPPLICATION

I stretch starved hands through the night,
Praying for tenderness.
Mary! From your calm height,
Pity my loneliness!
Incline a heart to loving-kindness.
Which strikes me dead of cold, because of blindness.

THE WIFE'S SONG.—I

I would carry you in my arms,
My strong One,
As if you were a child;
Over the long grass plains by the sea,
Where dunes are piled.

In the grey light of day that is late
Against wind from the sea I would carry your weight.
Till my body faint, but for love's control,
My soul will not faint to carry your soul.

I, who so weak had fallen to Hell
Carry my load, and ray Love's load well.

Old Sea, let us be steadfast!
New Hills give us hope of change!
Wind from the sea, cleanse us!
And you— O Pain, and Heaviness,
Sanctify me! Sanctify me!

THE WIFE'S SONG.—II

Two gifts I gave you, Love and Sorrow,
Of which the last is best.
But O, my Dear! 'Twas bitter giving.
Come here to me and rest.

What victory shall your world deny you.
Now you have wept?
All peace of love I will restore you
When you have slept.

CREATRIX

Let us thank Almighty God
For the woman with the rod.
Who was ever and is now
Strong essential as the plough.
She shall goad and she shall drive.
So to keep man's soul alive.
Amoris with her scented dress
Beckons, in pretty wantonness;
But the wife drives, nor can man tell
What hands so urge, what powers compel.

THE SHREW

You wish, O master of my destiny.
That I control myself!
'Twere better you ruled me.
For if I rule myself, I smile at you, and hate.
If you rule me, I love you though I curse, O mate!

REWARD

There is great gain.
Of pride and pain:
Let me be proud to claim the highest for my own
Let me bear pain, to fight my claim alone.

THE SAD LOVER

I weep for happy-sweet days
When your love was near me
Strong in its magical ways.
To hold and cheer me!

To my sad broken life,
Your love had given,
For endless, hopeless strife,
Peace of high Heaven.

I thought your charmed cure
Could have no ending.
And shall no spell endure
Of your dear befriending?

As a dead miser yearns
For earth-stored treasure.
So fiercely my soul burns
For old sweet pleasure.

Chilled by the bitter power,
Of sodden sinning
I find no splendid hour
As at love's beginning.

Now that my faith is weak,
Fearful I meet you!

Like a shy stranger speak.
When joy should greet you.

I deep in sorrow sing.
My passion proving,
"There is one beautiful thing.
Your tender loving."

Weep! Weep! for happy-sweet days,
When your love was near me.
Come from your solitary ways,
To hold and cheer me.

THE ARTIFICER

I feel that your neglect has flayed my soul
And left it a sore, bleeding, pulsing whole!
I feel there is hot fire in pain,
To boil the iron-pot that is my brain!

All my experience, all my thoughts and dreams.
Bubble together, and the mixture steams;
In lovely shapes the bluey vapours rise,
Angels and kindly goddesses console my eyes.

Into the boiling pot I plunge my spoon.
And of hot misery receive my boon.
For from the viscid liquor make I shapes.
Fairies and goblins, little goats and apes.

Many-hued jewels, gem-like flowers.
Bright beads to count kind prayers and happy hours
Once from the pot a crystal sphere I wrought,
It was a new, clear, and quite splendid thought.

NECROMANCY

If she could take two types of man,
Man that she loves, and man that she desires,
And fuse them in a magic pan,
Over the holy fires,
She might by Sorcery discover
A perfect Lover.

But she must build her Paradise above her.
Inherit Heaven after she is old.
For she can find no pleasant Love to love her,

The world is void of pleasure, and death-cold.

THE RECOMPENSE

Of every step I took in pain
I had some gain.
Of every night of blind excess
I had reward of half-dead idleness.
Back to the lone road
With the old load!
But rest at night is sweet
To wounded feet.
And when the day is long,
There is miraculous reward of song.

FLAGELLANT

Happiness is like a kind wife,
Within her rounded arms, she carries Sleep.
But I who am mad for Ecstasy, would keep
The favour of my mistress, Sorrow, all my life.

For Sorrow's sake,
Through the dark hours I lie awake.
So that my songs shall greet a day.
Which has forgot the pleasures of my clay.

THE STORMY MOON

I said, "I cannot look at beauty.
For I am heavy with desire;
I cannot touch this child's sweet hair.
My hand is fire."
O! I was desolate,
Burned dry and white.
Shut out from all kind comfort.
In the hungry night.

I did not heed the dark about me.
My head was bowed.
A scurrying wind came down and smote me.
Till I remembered cloud.
I raised my eyes to a wild cloud-drift.
And saw the travelling Moon.
Beauty and cold were so restored me.

And peace came soon.

WORDS

There came a lazy Celt,
Sunny and gay.
And he caused black ice to melt
With the things that he did say.

He said, "O! My Desire,
Behold your Lover stands.
His heart a cage of fire;
Come! Warm cold hands."

He said, "O! My Delight,
Be happy and be brave.
Weep no more for fright.
For I am a cave.

And I am kind and warm
And shut from icy air,
Where you shall find no harm
But live like a small brown bear.

O! Shelter in me, Sweet,
And let me give you rest.
For I love your hair and your feet.
And your pleasant moving breast."

ABDICATION

O judgment sleep!
I love an unkind thief.
Let me be friend of Frailty
For my sick heart's relief.

I would be as the shore's sand
Subject to an advancing sea,
I would be as sunken land
Swept by a tide's strong mastery.

But my contemning mind is as a lighthouse tower,
And I am sore for strength, and lashed because of power.

ASEPTIC

To live on a sterile hill
Suits not my mood,
I'll walk in towns my fill.
With strong resisting blood.

There is no virtue in stark fear,
Whether it be of Sin or Death,
But there is pride in walking clear,
Through Plague's contaminating breath.

DIVORCE

A voice from the dark is calling me.
In the close house I nurse a fire.
Out in the dark, cold winds rush free.
To the rock heights of my desire.
I smother in the house in the valley below,
Let me out to the night, let me go, let me go!

Spirits that ride the sweeping blast,
Frozen in rigid tenderness,
Wait! For I leave the fire at last.
My little-love's warm loneliness.
I smother in the house in the valley below,
Let me out to the night, let me go, let me go!

High on the hills are beating drums.
Clear from a line of marching men
To the rock's edge the hero comes.
He calls me, and he calls again.
On the hill there is fighting, victory, or quick death,
In the house is the fire, which I fan with sick breath.
I smother in the house in the valley below,
Let me out to the dark, let me go, let me go!

NERVOUS PROSTRATION

I married a man of the Croydon class
When I was twenty-two.
And I vex him, and he bores me
Till we don't know what to do!
It isn't good form in the Croydon class
To say you love your wife,
So I spend my days with the tradesmen's books
And pray for the end of life.

In green fields are blossoming trees
And a golden wealth of gorse,
And young birds sing for joy of worms:
It's perfectly clear, of course.
That it wouldn't be taste in the Croydon class
To sing over dinner or tea:
But I sometimes wish the gentleman
Would turn and talk to me!

But every man of the Croydon class
Lives in terror of joy and speech.
"Words are betrayers," " Joys are brief"—
The maxims their wise ones teach—
And for all my labour of love and life
I shall be clothed and fed.
And they'll give me an orderly funeral
When I'm still enough to be dead.

I married a man of the Croydon class
When I was twenty-two.
And I vex him, and he bores me
Till we don't know what to do!

And as I sit in his ordered house,
I feel I must sob or shriek.
To force a man of the Croydon class
To live, or to love, or to speak!

THE FIRED POT

In our town, people live in rows.
The only irregular thing in a street is the steeple;
And where that points to, God only knows,
And not the poor disciplined people!

And I have watched the women growing old.
Passionate about pins, and pence, and soap.
Till the heart within my wedded breast grew cold.
And I lost hope.

But a young soldier came to our town.
He spoke his mind most candidly.
He asked me quickly to lie down.
And that was very good for me.

For though I gave him no embrace—
Remembering my duty—
He altered the expression of my face.
And gave me back my beauty.

RETROSPECT

Your talk was most in praise of these poor features,
And of my body—not unequalled 'mongst God's creatures.
And even did your courteous fancy find
Some small perfection in a woman's mind.
But of my soul, sir, not a word!
Till your quite reasonable anger stirred
To bring our love to sudden wreck.
'Twas then you stayed my ecstasies
With truth! Which ended in this wise:—
"Woman! Your soul's a stone about your neck."

Maybe our love had happier consummation
Had this part known more quick consideration!

THE PIONEER

God send that never I speak truth again!
It's too strong meat for these most silly men!
God send that never in my life I lie!
God give me blessed silence till I die!

TRADUCERS

Kinder the enemy who must malign us,
Than the smug friend who will define us.

THE CHOICE

Two lovers wooed a woman.
The first was very kind and courtly, and he said—
"I offer you my honourable name,
And all the things there are to do, I do,
And everything you wish for I will give,
And you will be my lady, I your knight."

But the other smiled and said—
"Our love is late, I have no house to offer you,
But one good gift— yourself.
And you shall walk with me without constraint.
And all your words my wit shall understand,

And when our eyes meet full, we two shall smile.
And you will be my woman, I your man.
And you shall serve me."
Then the woman came softly to that man's side, and sat her down.

THE PROMISE

I will not love you for my duty,
Nor for all your treasure.
But I will love because of beauty.
And because of pleasure.
The boy that I shall bear will be a love-child.
Conceived in holy blindness,
I give him to the world who shall be reconciled
To loving-kindness.
Since I no longer love for duty.
Nor for all man's treasure,
And since I bear the child to Beauty
Because of pleasure.

THE ASSIGNATION

Gentlemen came wooing me
From north, east, west and south.
And each was afire
With quick desire
With a hot kiss on his mouth;
And there was never joy for me
From this dun, dull democracy.

My King, O my Delight!
Who is so strangely dear.
Kiss me not to-night.
Kiss me not for a year.
Let us live lonely days.
Keeping a holy fast.
Walking rough hilly ways.
So that we meet at last,
Near fir-trees on a height.
In still, kind, perfect night.

CEREMONY

Bring her rare unguents, and clear scented water,
And a golden gown, fit for a king's white daughter.

Bring mounds of flowers that she may spill about.
And herbs to make sweet smoke ere she goes out.
The victor is this maid's delight.
And he keeps tryst to night.

SERVICE

I love you so entirely
I cannot think to please you.
My art is wasted.
You are burnt with madness,
My being burns to ease you.
In dreams of utter service
Is all sweetness tasted.

I love you so entirely,
I want you not to praise me!
I would be low in all esteem!
I would be outcast with one thing to l'aise me,

The hope of service I have gathered in a dream.
Let us go to the mountains, O my Lover!
And make our habitation near the sky;
In clear, cool air we can discover
A plan of perfect living, you and I.

THE CRUEL LOVER

I ask your pardon that your pain
Should be so quick your lover's gain.
But when I know your love's distress.
My heart leaps high with happiness.
It sends kind tincture to my lips,
I walk with a new rhythm . . . from the hips.

REMEMBRANCE

What shall I do with my marriage dress?
In which I walked the lover's way.
Shall I wear it in forgetfulness,
Through a less honoured day?
Shall fastenings he has drawn for his delight,
Be loosed by a less honoured hand, at night?

STATE ENDOWMENT

Flowers all natural sweet,
That women sell on baskets in the street,
Lose half their beauty in my eyes.
They are a huckster's merchandise.

Who offers then to buy from me
That natural service, my maternity?

ORDEAL

I can endure the blight of drought
And the black rigour of my wild,
But not the name of Beauty on his mouth
And not to see him with a child.

THE FAITHFUL MOTHER

I could not be withheld from you by iron bands,
All cerements would be riven,
That we should claim our heaven.
But I am here in bondage, to these little, little hands!

If I unclasp the tender fingers and walk free,
Our love shall have no gain
From that poor hopeless pain,
For I shall lose my soul because of infamy.

O! Shall I walk your sunny gardens a cold ghost.
And will you cover me with flowers.
That I may spend sequestered hours.
Weeping the lovelier Blossoms I have lost!

I could not be withheld from you by iron bands.
All cerements would be riven,
That we should claim our heaven.
But I am here in bondage, to these little, little hands!

AFTER ANNUNCIATION

Rest, little Guest,
Beneath my breast.
Feed, sweet Seed,

At your need.
I took Love for my lord
And this is my reward.
My body is good earth.
That you, dear Plant, have birth.

A BOY'S MOUTH

His lips are open, since his mind
Delights in work his fingers find.
In that red arch I see a gate,
Where gracious Loves might pass in state.
Sure his white body were fit habitation
For a whole fairy population.

THE MOTHER-IN-LAW

This is what my lover said,
"I kissed your hat because it touched your head,
I kissed your shiny shoes, I'll kiss you all,
I love your house, I'll kiss your wall.
I wish that I could kiss that burning coal
Because it's in your fire, dear Soul!"

My little Son is my fond lover—
It seems no time ago since he was born.
I know he will be quick and happy to discover
The world of other women, and leave me forlorn!
Sometimes I think that I'll be scarcely human
If I can brook his chosen woman!

THE INDIVIDUALIST

When I get a child,
I get him with fixed intent,
I don't get him by accident.
I get him because I am content with life,
Satisfied with myself,
And because I love my wife.

When the child is born,
I am full of scorn.
At thought of other children.
By instinct I divine
There never was so fine a boy as mine.

I think this, because I am satisfied with life,
Conceited with myself.
And because I love my wife.

And I want to keep my son,
I want to finish what I have begun.
It is one of the keenest pleasures that I know
To feed a child and watch him grow.
I don't want to give him to the State,
I want to share him with my mate.
I like going into hustling life.
To bring back something for my boy and wife.

I do this because the old Brave
Hunted from the cave.
Because a lion in the wilderness
Kills for the cub and lioness.
And because I am satisfied with life.
Conceited with myself.
And because I love my wife.

THE WALK

We will walk through this wood,
Rustling through dead leaves,
Crunching on fallen boughs,
I will walk first, you must follow me.
We will go like beasts on a trail.
I am a lion, you my lioness.

I will take my own pace.
You must strain your curved brittle body to keep near me.
I do this because I see in your eyes that you will talk.
O wanton! You will stab me with subtleties.
I have no head for economics. What of that?
Your eyes, your hair, your teeth, your body,
You have used against me,
And now your mind is a sharp sword to stab me.

I want to walk in this wood.
To look at the sky, and note the tracery of leaves.
And listen for an early cuckoo.
But you will have me sit beside you.
Tell you that you are a beautiful woman,
And praise your wit.

I will not tell you that you are a beautiful woman.
You are my wife!
You know well that I feel every stir of you.

Can you not remember the touch of my hand on your arm?"
I will say nothing at all about your wit.
But I will tell you this,
I think it very possible, that one of our sons.
Yours and mine, will be a man of genius.

O Jezebel! I see the triumph leap to your eyes.
You love your children less than yourself.
Are you the only parent of our son?
Did not my love make you mother?
Did I not know from the first moment that I saw you.
Your splendid suitability?

That act of mine means more to life
Than all your economics.
You shall not waste your time with books!
I will have other sons of you, and perhaps a girl.
I will tell you that your daughter is beautiful.

Now look at me!
This only matters to us.
You are a woman, I am male.
I am male till the last atom of my tissue dies.—
Come now, walk!

ALL MEN TO WOMEN

You have taken our life in your hands, like a small sick bird;
As you might feed him with your lips, so with your word
Have you sustained us; remembering your kind eyes
We have forgot our pitiless ways, and have grown wise.

With brittle strength to fight and to desire.
What do we but bring fuel to your fire?
For our best labour, your fine powers control,
O maker of man's body and his soul!

The flower of all our winning we would give
To mightier men, the Race that is to live.
On your good courage must our victory rest,
You bear all future days beneath your breast.

There are those among you who scorn their trust.
Who have betrayed us, being weak to lust.
Cursed be our weakness, cursed be that deceit.
For that black sin, is no good thing complete.

O pitiful heart! From whom we draw our strength.
Would you have wisdom? Know your power at length.

From your frail might grant us the thing we seek.
We who are born so small, and live so weak.

A GIRL IN SUMMER

She took the summer to her blood
Through her sweet mouth.
Until her sleepy mood
Was warm as sunny walls of the old south.
It seemed the yellow light
Had fruitful powers,
Beneath her bosom's white
Leapt sudden flowers.
Each round as the breast
From whose dear core it sprang,
And in the middle of each flower a nest,
In which a young bird sang;
Sang for joy of a coming
And for joy of a name,
And the petals of the flower
Leapt like flame.
Driving with a sweet compelling
Towards his dwelling,
As her singing birds were telling.

THE ANCHORITE

Ye Chaste, who nurse your souls upon chill heights,
What can you give us but a dead world?

I have walked too long in the strait road,
I have kept my limbs from the dance,
I have flung no songs to the Stars.
What have I for my stillness, but a tale of things undone!

Rather had I borne the common yoke.
Better had I made a fellow of Sin
Than win this sterile victory.

O! moving Powers inflame me.
Lead me to some brave combat,
Though then you throw me to deep Hell
With one full memory.

Now I surrender a pale heaven
Of unbegotten spirits, and of unfilled days.

THE SONG-MAKER

I would live for a day and a night.
In the rigorous land where everything is right.
Then I would sit and make a song,
In the leisurely land where everything's wrong.

IMPERATRIX

Am I pleasant?
Tell me that, old Wise!
Let me look into your eyes.
To see if you can comprehend my beauty.
That is a lover's duty.
I look at you to see
If you can think of anything but me.
Ah, you remember praise and your philosophy!
My love shall be a sphere of silence and of light,
Where Love is all alone with love's delight.—
Here is a woodcutter who is so weak
With love of me, he cannot speak.
Tell me, dumb man, am I pleasant, am I pleasant?
Farewell, philosopher! I love a peasant.

SONG OF ANASTASIA

Shall I mock you, and tell you that love shall endure.
Knowing you know the quality of things that are secure.''
Let love be fierce as lightning, and as brief
As summer-hail, that is a storm's relief.

QUESTION

If I live all my days by routine,
Keeping days ordered and ways clean,
Will there be room for Love in my life?
Love who is born in storm, and lives in strife.

THE CONSCIENCE

Deadly destructive to my man and me

Are my rare fits of sore morality.
A mad domestic hell begins
When woman hides her virtues, and displays her sins.

SONG OF THE WEAK

O pitying heart be strong!
Our load is heavy and the road is long,
And there is little light to cheer our day
And little kindness on the mourner's way.

RELEASE

I have lived five years of mourning,
I live a bitterer year of scorning.
Now of this service is my spirit free,
Free of my grief, and of antipathy.

THE CONTRAST

I knew a pure man, who was without pity,
I knew the veriest bawd in all this city.
And she was very tender, very kind—
She was most after God's mind.

TATTERDEMALION

O I will wear a tattered gown
And ash my breast shall cover,
For my bird has gone to the clanging town.
To the hand of my valiant lover!
But still myself shall sit and sing.
By the bed of the old blind king.

O! If I stept in bright array,
And bound my hair with beauty
I'd follow my bird to a feckless day
And leave this dearer duty.
In ash I'll sit, in rags I'll sing.
By the bed of the old blind king.

THE GHOST

I wish you'd a farm on the hills, my Dear,
And need not work for hire.
For though I'm cold in the churchyard here.
And cannot sit by your fire,
I'd walk the paths of your house, some nights.
And haply look into your room:
Then I'd always see my Love's home-lights
When I stood on the rail of my tomb.

WOMEN AND MULTITUDES

When weak knave commanded me.
Then I was stung to mutiny!
But when my king spoke his behest.
In quick obedience I found rest.
Now to the dark I cry my need,
"God send us kings, to love, and lead."

THE WOMAN'S MIND

Knowledge to me is wearisome from books,
I learn so readily from words and looks.
Give me yourself as free as air and rain.
I'll drink, I'll think, and send you flowers again.

SELF-ESTEEM

Love with a liquid ecstasy
Did wholly fill me up,
And since his drink is sweet to me
Can I despise his cup?"

THE AVENUE

To the tired traveller in summer's heat.
The thought of airy trees is sweet.
Come, in my straight stretched arms discover
A leafy road, thou weary Lover.

THE SOLACE

Since pleasure is a sovereign cure
How can my piteous pain endure?
To-night I hide my face in your dress,
O Font of Peace! O Healing Tenderness!

WARNING

The soul shall be drowned in the flood
Of mounting blood.
Be strong at least
To resist Love,
Except at his feast.

ETERNAL SONGS

I am a field spread warm before the sun—
Lord of my day! Your love is warmth and light.
In me all growth and pleasure are begun:
A bird soars singing to salute your height.
Love, my fond words,
Are happy birds!

I am the sun's self,
And you the waters of a still bright lake;
My arms encircling airs,
Which draw you, drink you, for my sun-ship's sake.

THE WOMAN OF THE HILL

I would be ever your desired,
Never the possessed—
Nor in this will of mine is wantonness expressed.
The desired woman is most dear,
The possessed wanton is too near.

I would be far on unattainable height—
Always for knowledge, always for sight:
While from your touch aud kisses I am free.
Our love is the high, perfect thing to be.

OASIS

Sweet Spring of my Content,
The parching days are spent.
Where'er your feeding waters move
There is the sweet increase of love.

I, wanderer in a wilderness
Starved of all hope and comfortless,
Now lay me down in groves of cool delight
Which you have nurtured, in a charmed night.

THE MEETING

When I saw you, you went to my head.
You were like wine to my brain,
I walked in London through the rain,
To see a man who had been ten years dead.
For pleasure I forgot the years.
Old time, old death, old tears.

THE LITTLE LANGUAGE

When I am near you, I'm like a child,
I am still and simple, I am undefiled.
I speak my love in a forgotten tongue.
And use the words I knew when I was young.
My Love! You have restored me in a hundred ways,
You gave me back my happy childish days.

VANITY

I saw old Duchesses with their young Loves,
I, in a pair of very shabby gloves,
Even my shapeless garments could not make me sad,
For I remembered I was young as you, dear Lad.
That I am lovelier without my dress
Gave me sweet wanton happiness.

THE WALK IN THE WOODS

High Heaven is insecure.
Give me my paradise while these warm arms endure.
Come, my Love! let us walk in this brake.

Where I can see you sleep, and watch you wake.
So much of perfect pleasure, for Mortality's poor sake.

INVOCATION

Come down, thou friendly Night
Drive out this traitor Light,
Who will reveal my silent way!
And Darkness give me cover,
That I may find my Lover,
After the fevered day!

IRRESOLUTE LOVER

I said, "I will not go to her to-night,"
When I had courage from the prudent light.
My resolution vanished with the day,
When the dark came I could not live away.

O! My dear Love let down your hair,
Make me a tent, and let me shelter there;
That in the darkness of a screened night
I live more prudent than in loveless light.

A MAN IN LOVE

I wish no more that beauty walked in light
Utterly naked to the daily sight.
Rather let some sweet simple dress
Shelter my Woman's loveliness.
So is her beauty love's high prize,
Which I discover with adoring eyes.

THE SILENCE

When I meet you, I greet you with a stare;
Like a poor shy child at a fair.
I will not let you love me—yet am I weak.
I love you so intensely that I cannot speak.
When you are gone, I stand apart.
And whisper to your image in my heart.

FEAR

By your sweet love am I restored,
But ask me not for love's reward.
I am full of love as is a cloud
Pregnant with thunders long and loud.
I tremble, for in this wild sky
Are lightnings, by which man may die!

THE FLIGHT

I fear your sight
O Lover!
I make the night
My cover.
I know your touch a dreaded thing;
I go to sombre woods to sing;
Where you are not is such a sick distress
That I must sing a lover's loneliness!
But if my songs shall lead you where I hide,
Then have I silence, now so long denied.

SLAVE OF THE FIRE

I am weary of my service to the blood of a king.
For my people were farmers out of the West,
I would be wife of this yeoman of whom my heart sings,
In his strong love, I would take my rest.
O I That I might raise a man to my kind.
Shelter him in my womb, and feed him with my mind.

THE SUPREME COURTESY

My man is like a good steel blade.
As subtle, strong, and finely made,
His power blue-white
As steely light.
O, he is cruel-quick enough!
But to my touch, as pleasant as fine stuff.
And from a wound of him I'd die,
Happy at such keen mastery.

THE FAREWELL

Tonight
For the last time,
I loose my hair to make a tent about you.
Come lay your head on my knees.
Your eyes are the lights of a town.
And my body is a sheltering hill.
Now my hair is a cloud.
To hide you from the inquisitive stars.

REGRET

After a grey day's forgetting
Was the red of this sun's setting.
And the ache of my regretting.

To-night my bed is a rack,
I die painful for love's lack . . .
O! My Beloved, come back! come back!

SURRENDER

When you kiss me I am blind,
My senses
Are filled with ecstasy.
I only feel how strong my life is,
And so know myself.
From love I understand all things that live,
And even the dead.

I am like a tree
Shaken in wind.
Or like water that is drawn into the air
Through the strong loving of the sun.

When you are gone,
I am myself earthquake and eclipse,
And all cold darkness, and rending grief.
When you kiss me I am blind.
I am blind!

THE MILL

I hid beneath the covers of the bed,

And dreamed my eyes were lovers,
On a hill that was my head.

They looked down over the loveliest country I have seen,
Great fields of red-brown earth hedged round with green.
In these enclosures I could see
The high perfection of fertility,

I knew there were sweet waters near to feed the land,
1 heard the churning of a mill on my right hand,
I woke to breathlessness with a quick start,
And found my mill the beating of your heart.

THE CUP

I dreamed that all your being was a cup,
Shaped like the upheld hands of an adoring priest.
I dreamed that loving had transposed my blood to wine
I scented the wine with my low-whispered songs,
So the red liquor was Love's self—

Then with an ecstasy I spilled myself into the cup.

My soul was driven from my body
And waited watching like pearl-coloured flame,
That flame was prayer,
I prayed you might contain me.

If the arching fulness of the cup be broken,
If Love shall overflow the cup
And fall like blood from a wound,
Then shall my soul's light die.

O, Man, contain me!

SUNG OF CLARISSA

Why is there healing in her love?''
Her mind is clear as streams that flow
Down rock-steps to a vale below.
Bearing on spray the Sun's bright bow.
And singing as they move.

WANDER SONG

When I come to the end of the land,
I find the sea.
With edges of cliff and breadths of sand
To pleasure me.

When I raise my town-tired eyes
There is blue and white,
Or kings and castles of stormy skies.
Or joy of night.

When I weary of all I see
And tire even of space,
I hold your love in memory
And your dear face.

THE THIEF

I said in pride, "To love's my need;
I will not have him loving me,
I'd walk unhobbled, and indeed
What woman loved was ever free!"

So for a man, I loved a ghost.
And knew chill rapture in the walks of thought,
But when I needed pleasure most,
Imagination gave me naught.

O! Had I given what I fought to take
I had not wept for this cold hunger's sake!

REVELATION

"Love has no shame."—
'Twas this you said to me.
Shall Love reveal
Hid beauties that are real
And still disguise the soul's infirmity
In fear of blame?
"Love has no cruelty."—
See first the wounds that are within
Hidden by this quite sufficient skin.
Loving your spirit, I may not deceive it.
Then of my body, Lover—take or leave it.

SEA TO THE WANING MOON

O thou compassionate queen of night!
With what a kind inconstancy
Thou wanest upon my hopeless sight
To leave me with a memory!

What spite to me who cannot climb,
To see you ever at night's prime,
Compelling with sweet silent speech.
Ever desirous, ever out of reach!

TRANSMUTATION

There is happiness for me.
In sight of a great sun-warmed tree.
I pray that roots may touch my head,
When I am dead.

Maybe there is some splendid compound rhythm in confusion,
And there is hope in dissolution.
I should have little fear of ugly changes, little grief.
If the material of my thought were quick transmuted to a leaf.

A HOUSE IN HAMPSTEAD

My house is damp as damp can be,
It stands on London clay.
And if I move unthinkingly
It shakes in a most alarming way,
Mayhap it will all come down on me
One day.
But through the window I can see
The most enchanting apple-tree.
In spring-time, there are daffodils
And primroses on little hills,
And high within my apple-tree
A blackbird comes and sings to me;
On the black branch he sits and sings
Of birds and nests and eggs and things.
I can't remember as I hear—
That old grey London lies so near.

THE AWAKENING

There is a veteran tree,

With green-stained bark,
Rising like a tower of the sea.
From the smooth park.
He is a giant among trees,
And he has watched this house for centuries.

His bark is hard as rock,
Time and Sun and the Wind's shock
Have twisted his boughs till they are like the arms of a great carven figure of Care,
Flung in passionate appeal to the changing humour of the Air.
Now on high branches sticky buds appear,
Promise of growth and beauty for the year.—
It seems my life is an old tree,
And the young buds are your sweet love for me.

THE TRESPASSER

There is a little goblin in my tree.
He sits up high and mows at me.
He is so wicked, yet so small.
He makes my garden venturous, and my trees tall.

CONCERNING CERTAIN CRITICISM

There is no pleasure in hard names for flowers,
Nor in acquaintance with their inner shape.
To ravish Beauty with dividing powers
Is to let exquisite essences escape.
At feasts within a flowery paradise
Parvenu Wit must yield his precedence,
Honours therein are for the nose and eyes,
For that old exquisite, discerning sense.

THE EXPLAINERS

They have taken the street
From underneath my feet,
Now the great roads appear
Unmeaning scratches on a sphere.
They have given every star its place.
They have made a wearying diagram of what was boundless space.
Long ago they stole fairies from the trees,
They took naiads from the rivers, and mermen from the seas.
I wish that I could tremble now
In fear of a small devil curled upon that bough.

In these imaginings I should find
Relief from the strained stillness, that is my mind.

FAITH

I keep a bird in my heart,
He lives on sorrow,
His name is Faith.
He is so quick a conjurer that he can borrow
Flesh from a wraith.

He swallows the harsh weeds of pain
And gives me scope,
To tend my little garden-plot again
And wait for Hope.

INSENSIBILITY

Why should I weep for Autumn rain?
Give gusty Winter toll of tears?
I know that Spring will come again,
As in the other years.

And there is pleasure in wet ways.
In frozen fields, and mist-strange days;
What were eternal Spring to me,
Whose joy is in diversity!

CONCERNING THE CONVERSATION OF MR H—

This gentleman will only talk to us of dogs
Because he wishes to disguise that he's a poet,—
If he should mention lions, dolphins, frogs,
He thinks by misadventure, we should know it!

He tells us things of white dogs, and of brown,
Of curious breed with one distinctive spot.
Of all the dogs that ever walked this town.
Of dogs of his acquaintance that have not.

I cite a dog I once set eyes upon
Which, lacking doggy lore, I say looked like a swan;
He takes me, says, " That hound was bred in Russia,
Three such are owned by Henry, Prince of Prussia."

O, modest violet! cowering in your green
Your scent betrays you though you are not seen!
Only unveterinary wights, like you and me,
Would see in dogs a swanny quality!

TO ANITA THE BOUNTIFUL MOTHER

O generous woman! gracious and so kind—
Take a long-needed rest of body and of mind.
You gave so many gifts of service and of sympathy
Can you refuse this gift of gifts to me?
Now I desire no food, no garment, and no rose
But the sweet sight of your most calm repose.

THE PASSER

I love the stone of your threshold,
I love the path without it,
I love the briar in its borders,
With the brave young plants about it.
There is pleasure in sight of your windows.
And passing, in decorous night
I smile my love to your window
And bow my love to your light.

THE SENTIMENTAL DEBTOR

Lady, when I recall indebtedness
To you who hid me from my bitter day,
And with kind craft bewitched my griefs away
I would not have my owing to you less!

Untimely night has fall'n between us two.
Mine were the blackness of a dumb regret
But for the dear relation of this debt.
Which still unites my destiny to you.

Thus in my cold a little cheer is found.
The fullest debt will hold me fastest bound.
Here's coin for quittance, yet I will withhold
Return in any service, faith or gold.
And since your due is doubly dear to me,
I will not even give you courtesy!

THE DEPENDENCE

I am your shadow, since I love,
'Tis you compel my changing mood.
Now to be still, and now to move.
You are my evil and my good.
Smile, Lady, and behold in me.
The grace of mirrored courtesy!

THE BARGAINER

The clownish reveller is driven hence.
I meet no night with frenzied amorous waste
Nor drug my noon with self-deceiving haste.
This to your light, my reasoned reverence.

Now since I love, I am content with Time.
I scorn that impotent mad will to cause;
Trusting the gradual action of old laws.
To round my life, and to mature my rhyme.

O! You, who are the worker of this change.
Respect in me the measure of your power.
Hold to a steady godhead, lest I range
From growing symmetry of this new hour!
If Chaos wake from shattered Harmony,
Yours be the shame of half divinity.

TO ANITA THE GARDENER

In summer when my life was cold,
Frozen too weary for desire,
I warmed my heart at your marigold,
As at a fire.

It was the first flower from your new ground,
The first gold largess from the care
And loving, you had planted there.
And in the walks around.

I stole your garden's coin to buy content,
A vision of black earth dug deep for flowers.
Through sunny self-forgetful hours,
With joys, God meant.

In summer when my life was cold.

Frozen too weary for desire,
I warmed my heart at your marigold.
As at a fire.

THE CALL

Walk out, my Love, from little houses.
From these dim walls of old restraints.
Heavy with odorous griefs and melancholy plaints,
Cobwebbed with sighs.
Let us find a field where a quiet cow browses,
A field wind-swept to clean content.
And we will love there as God meant,
Under free skies.

VERITY

What do these outpoured lovings prove
But the long ache to love!
O Fate! You are not kind,
To fill this chasm with cold wind.
When had a woman wealth from dreaming.
Or any solace for love's seeming?
Let it be said, that these are dexterous feignings.
Well stated heats, ingenious complainings.
And yet with loathing is my silence broken.
Had they been true, they never had been spoken.
What fuller happiness were it for me.
To leave a mummer's rages
To fill a footnote in my Love's biography.
And not these loving pages.

EPICUREAN LOVER

Dear! I will love you, though you love me not!
Contempts will never shake my mind!
Misuse and scorn and silence move me not I
But I beseech you, be not kind.
Since loving me, you would approach me,
O, let your distance still reproach me!

For things remembered may be sweet.
As things imagined, and for me
A wearying rhythm of due feet
Were less esteemed than your apostasy.

Then, O my Love! Live still beyond my reach.
Leave me my dream of your dear look and speech.

THE POET'S CHANGE OF MIND

Who prizes fruit and scorns the tree?
Yet this fair Critic says of me,
I love the work, but hate the man!
Show charier charity who can!

My Lady, I was ever loth
To wait inactive to be loved,
I found in insult, whips from sloth,
When I was stung I moved.
But there is justice for whose sake
A sleepy dignity will wake.
If of my book you prize a part.
Honour a hand, deal fairly with a heart.
The thing you love is very me,
Come, eat the fruit, but love the tree!

DIFFIDENCE

O time has a kiss
For every Miss
And a bed for every Trull!
But thou, my Dearie,
O! Come not near me,
Our love is a wheeling gull.
Lovely he flies 'twixt sea and skies.
He's a silly bird on land.
No wrath of black weathers
Will ruffle his feathers
Like the touch of a capturing hand.

TO "NUCLEUS"

'Tis you who hold
My heat, my cold,
My rigour and my ecstasy.
Control my days,
Compel my ways
To action or to lethargy.
You fill my nights
With keen delights

Of a stupendous dreaming.
O! Little Seed,
Who at my need
Flowers to such splendid seeming

THE NEOPHYTE

I carry thoughts of you
As I might wear a charm.
These are my Scapular
Clothing me from harm.

You lock ray lips
With a most cunning key,
And all my heart
Is your still oratory.

ABSOLUTE

I, your true lover,
Demand neither words nor your silence.
My heart can discover
Delight in transport or in continence.

My faith is zenith, earth, and air,
Ever beneath, about, above.
And when you wander I am there,
So changing-constant—since I love.

THE FALLOW

Now, Tiller, hold your grain.
Leave her to sun and rain
And the kind air.
Then trench her with a well-judged measure
Of feeding pleasure,
And give her peace
To dream of her increase
And your good care.
Well might you reap miraculous yield
From such a happy, nourished field!

HOMMAGE ETERNEL

To Anita: 14a Downshire Hill, Hampstead.

Hygenia's house gave space for dreaming
And a small place for sleeping,
With laughter for a soul's redeeming
And sweet release of weeping.
Within her walls Disorder's daughter,
Dusty, devoid of hope,
Found unction in kind offered water
And various sorts of soap.

THE RETURN

She gave me tears,
A rain to wash the dust of years,
A silence for disharmony.
For jagged wounds a remedy.
Green windy downs for foetid towns
For slums sweet-scented closes.
And for the thorn of her blest scorn
I gave her thorny roses.

THE WINDED HORN

Ah! my good Wizard she shall not escape.
Though the soul leave her house in a magical shape.
Be it asp, toad or lizard, or tiger or ape,
Sure I will find her, secure I will bind her,
Wherever she fly, in whatever disguise.
I am Love the hunter, all-swift and all-wise,
A torch is my hand and spears are my eyes.

THE LITTLE ROOM

I am my Love's laboratory,
For truly he shall find
The proof of his high quality
Within my heart and mind.
Look down, my Love, my Dear,
At the sure change wrought here!

MODERN ANOMALIES

When a Man and his Wife are watching a KINEMATOGRAPH.

Many a time, seeing their darkened house at close of day
She opened that dear gate, and knelt upon their steps to pray.
And through their window crannies crept her loving powers,
Till all their dwelling smelt of blessing, as a wood of flowers.

THE ECONOMIST

It must be true I love you well
Since your light words are whips of Hell.
But who has pain has songs to sell.
My profitable Friends, farewell!

INCONSTANCY

Time was, when I recalled your words, your looks, your deeds.
As a rapt nun counts over her blest Beads;
Then was my mind so filled with memory
Love had no room to work his change in me,
And I was faithless from my faith's continuance.
Since being changeless I gave no obedience.

I have forgotten you, for these long days,
All unsustained by you I went my ways,
Now at the end I take you back to thought
To find my action was the thing you taught.
And so in faithlessness is faith's continuance,
Since in a change I do you all obedience.

SONG

Not for an hour shall your dear thought escape me.
I keep it fast to cheer, to guide, to shape me.
As an old pilot held in sight a star.
As a wrecked man clings frantic to a spar.
So I maintain your love in memory,
My hope of Heaven, my security.

THE POET

Here is he, at this moment, which is Time's end,

Lonely as he was born, without a friend.
And he has called the hungry to his door,
And he has shared his bounty with the poor.
He has been feasted, he has been desired,
Lovers have drunk of him, till they were tired.
All men have ate his councils and passed by.
Thankless, as who shall thank the sky.

FOR PITY

Men are brought low by blame.
So that they live with shame.
Kindness and love and praise
Are strong to heal and raise.

PRAYER FOR MIRACLE

O God! No more Thy miracle withhold.
To us in tents give palaces of gold,
And while we stumble among things that are
Give us the solace of a guiding star!

DE PROFUNDIS

How shall I bring this beast into subjection
But by the hope and knowledge of perfection?
Must I avoid all paths my Race has trod?
Shall I not call my vast upholder God?

THE TORTURE

God has raised his whip of Hell
That you be no longer weak.
Because of anguish shall you speak.
Because of anguish, shall you speak well.

SANCTUARY

He who thinks a perfect melody,
Lives for that time, in perfect harmony.
Walks for that time in liberty,

Loves for that time in purity.

IMMORTALITY

The Singer sang through all his years,
But thrifty Honour saved his tears.
And for his piteous toil,
Blessed him with weeping, as with Holy Oil.

"SUCH STUFF AS DREAMS ARE MADE OF"

A man can build a bridge of wood and stone;
Exterior forces his trained powers control;
But the material of the Singer is his own,
He cuts his songs out of the raw texture of his soul.

QUEST

Where is the miracle? In Future and in Past,
Not in the Present, which must ever last.
The Young and the weak Old must live dream-fed
On gods to be, and on the holy Dead.

THE SONG OF PRIDE

We are unwilling to lie low,
Crushed by a cursed tyrant "No."
Give us a fight where we can cry, "I can!"
To show there is the seed of God in man.
If God shall strike us for our pride
Know that in joy of death we died.

MY LADY SURRENDERS

How did she abdicate?
Was it with soft sighs
And pretty feignings of a lover's state,
Or was it solemn-wise.
With altar offerings and rapt vows?
O no! when Love himself was there,
Most housewifely she bound her hair

And went off across the field to milk the cows.

COUNSEL OF ARROGANCE

If I were God, I would find equal treasure,
In human work, in courage, and in pleasure.
And I would whisper to the captive soul,
That all these things should be in sweet control.
That man should be from birth-bed to the grave,
Not always busy, not always brave.
That he should gather me the flower of idleness.
And the seed-holding cup of perfect happiness.

PRAYER ON SUNDAY

God send a higher courage
For to cut straight and clean!
God send a juster language,
To state the thing I mean!
Here is such random thinking,
Such sloth, such slime, such fog,
I see an old cow sinking
Deep, in a pitchy bog!

EFFECT OF GIFTS ON A RECIPIENT

When the ape and the wolf bared fangs to eat
A silly dish of praise,
The drowsing master snatched the meat
Which mocked his faithless days.
He grasped the beasts by a hanging chain
And stood in his house, a lord again.
Then out he went through a feeble morn
With the drunken sleep in his eyes.
He begged affront, he craved for scorn,
In mendicant's disguise.
And of these gifts divinely given.
His faith in life, his hope of Heaven.

SUNG TO THE SOCIAL REFORMER

Leave us our sorrows,
Take not our tears,

For long to-morrows
Of too perfect years.

To the New-born can you deny
The world-old solace of a cry;
Nor to hot Youth the eternal right
To win his having with a fight.

Leave us our sorrows.
Take not our tears,
For long to-morrows
Of too perfect years.

THE JOURNEY

I have seen the harlot decked for death,
I have seen the fruitful woman scorned for ugliness.
I will not embrace Beauty but Order,
Scorning this body which must grow old.

I have heard the loveless laughter of fools,
I have seen the wanton and the pander drunk with mirth.
Laughter is a sacrament which should be shared for Love's sake.
Let us then be merry when mirth is no sacrilege.

I have seen the eyes of a smirched man turn from his paramour's lapdog
To find refreshment in a child's look.
So for a moment were his banned eyes filled with heavenly light.
Who seeing this, can still boast sterile loves?

THE VIPER

I heard a pander say in scorn of a bawd,
"A child should be her reward."
O, rotten speech!
Whose filthiness should teach
That man shall find
Reward for his lewd living, in his mind.

DOOM

Ye Slothful!
The hour of dread is upon you
When the perfect thing shall be accomplished.
The defiler of law

May meet God down avenues of hot sin.
You—performers of nothing
Who weave your little mats in damp valleys
What use had mighty God, or a strong devil, for your shrunk souls?
There is black Hell or clear Heaven for the souls of the Willers;
Surely there is an eternal scrap-heap for the souls of the
Slothful!
For the rejected of Heaven,
For the throw-outs of any incontemptible Hell.

OUTLAW

Suppression is the duty of a slave,
Expression is morality for the brave.
If you are born a king,
Fight, love, and sing!
But he who walks alone in liberty
Must face the hordes of massed humility.
Now, as of old, a leader risks his head,
A coward dies an inch a day, a hero is quick dead.

THE FRESH START

O give me back my rigorous English Sunday
And my well-ordered house, with stockings washed on Monday.
Let the House-Lord, that kindly decorous fellow,
Leave happy for his Law at ten, with a well-furled umbrella.
Let my young ones observe my strict house rules.
Imbibing Tory principles, at Tory schools.

Two years now I have sat beneath a curse
And in a fury poured out frenzied verse.
Such verse as held no beauty and no good
And was at best new curious vermin-food.

My dog is rabid, and my cat is lean.
And not a pot in all this place is clean.
The locks have fallen from my hingeless doors,
And holes are in my credit and my floors.

There is no solace for me, but in sooth
To have said baldly certain ugly truth.
Such scavenger's work was never yet a woman's.
My wardrobe's more a scarecrow's than a human's.

I'm off to the House-goddess for her gift.
"O give me Circumspection, Temperance, Thrift;

Take thou this lust of words, this fevered itching,
And give me faith in darning, joy of stitching I ''

When this hot blood is cooled by kindly Time
Controlled and schooled, I'll come again to Rhyme.
Sure of my methods, morals and my gloves,
I'll write chaste sonnets of imagined Loves.

DOMESTIC ECONOMY

I will have few cooking-pots,
They shall be bright,
They shall reflect to blinding
God's straight light.
I will have four garments,
They shall be clean,
My service shall be good,
Though my diet be mean.
Then I shall have excess to give the poor.
And right to counsel beggars at my door

THE MOCKER

No longer will I upbraid,
But go my way in silence!
From shame, I am afraid
And brought to my soul's continence!

I saw a man bowed 'neath a Dream,
Go painful, to ransom a city—
'Tis such alone will redeem.
And yet from him I withheld pity.—

But as a mocker I spoke,
"Good Ox, graze here, by the road,
'Tis an ignominious yoke
When dust is the load!"

And I saw in a ransomer's eyes
Ire, for God's purpose defamed.
God give me the gag of the wise—
I am shamed!

A SONG OF WOMEN

When Kings knelt to a Maid and a Child,
In a poor place that kings could scorn,
Was Might exalted in a Maid?
Or stark Strength praised in the New-born?

Then was a babe known as Earth's Lord,
And a maid's arm was God's strong shield,
How long shall this Woman wait her reward,
The honour that her love should yield?

Upraised in Churches shrined in Art,
Ages have seen a Girl and Child.
But fullest honour is for days.
When Life and Faith are reconciled.

When Love is counted strong as Strength,
And all the tongues of service speak.
When you in council hear at length
The guardians of your mighty weak.

What splendid empire can you build?''
What destiny in pride and lands.
That is not by our babes fulfilled
That is not in your women's hands.

Now we, the guardians of your Race,
Strong to fulfil your mighty task.
Ask in your Councils for our place,
And you will give us what we ask.

When Kings knelt to a Maid and a Child,
In a poor place that kings might scorn,
Then was our pleading justified.
By that strong Mother and her New-born.

THE FOUNDLING

There is a little naked child at the door,
His name is Beauty, and he cries,
"Behold, I am born, put me where I can live."
The old World comes to the door,
And thrusting out a lip, says only this,
"It is true that you are born, but how were you conceived?"

There is an owl upon an elder-tree,
Who opening an eye, says only this.
"That is a lovely child!"
The old World said again,
"Yes! but how was he conceived?"

There is a gust of free wind.
And high cloud voices call.
"What can you ask of Love but conception?
Men are born of blest love,
Of evil love is death.
There is but one pure love, the love of Child,
And that is sweet as a pine forest, clean as the sea:
Old World take all your children in."

THE TOWN DIRGE

A child was dead in the town,
Son of a sick woman and a poor man.
The woman being sick gave only her love.
And what can the poor man give!
A child was dead in the town.

In the house of our pity
The woman wept for her child.
But we, being wise, whispered apart,
"Seeing that the man is poor, and the woman sick,
It is well that the child is dead."

She, of her courtesy, asked us to look at her child,
But I could not enter the poor room,
I could not face its Dead.
My heart accused my lips and cried,
"No child should die."

O, you! Who are strong in the town.
Mighty to build, mighty to shield the weak,
Join with us that we may say.
Under God's grace, and of our good care,
No child shall die.

THE SONG OF THE CHILD

Receive me again, Father God,
There is no room!
There is war upon earth, men fight,
They have no time, no food, no pity for babes.
The women staunch men's wounds, and forget us.
Mothers with child are starved.
The new-born dies at the empty breast;
So I died who was your messenger.
I have made no beauty, I have spoke no truth,

I have failed, I was rejected, born too soon.
Receive me again! Father God! Receive me!

THEFT

When first I saw the old man dead,
I laid a curious hand upon his head,
To leave that little left in the soul's mould,
The knowledge of the rigour and the cold.
I asked no pardon of the Clay,
For the dead eyes had wandered in their day.
And kneeling ceremonious at his side,
I found a book he'd dropt the day he died.
Verses—which I repeated to dead ears in lieu of prayers,
I stole the book, regardless of his heirs,
Asking no pardon of the Clay
For the dead man had loved me in his day.

MATER DOLOROSA

The Mother of Mercy in sorrow wise
Looks at our wounds with her kind eyes,
Heals with her look, as the great scathless can;
In every man she sees a child, in every child a man.

Lo! her great spirit leaves the holy height,
Swoops to the depths where old Sin lies at night,
And the grey head to her good breast she takes.
And kisses lips that curse before the worn child wakes.

She, mortal woman, knew the stress of birth,
In a frail child she bore the King of Earth.
The eternal symbol of our faith she stands
Who put all hope into our Children's hands.

Mother of Mercy, in sorrow wise.
Look at our life with your kind eyes.
Charm our dull sight, as your sweet pity can,
To see in every man a child, in every child a man.

SOLITARY

When love is over, are we most alone.
When hearths are black, there is the cold of stone.
I rise from my bed and walk the dismal night.

Weeping I seek alone my ultimate right.

The warmth and cheer of Love is but a lure.
By which the blood is cheated to endure.
To each man is a path, by other feet untrod,
Which leads him, lonely, to the hill of God.

On God's cold hill, there is a holy height.
Where splendid fires descend to man at night:
On the cold traveller falls the livening breath.
To raise him high in life, and proud in death.

MISERERE MEI DEUS

God, I am broken, broken,
I have nothing left but my tears.
These are the wealth I have gathered
Through my tempestuous years,

I have trusted Life,
I have leaned on Love,
I have gone from hope to hope, in vain.
From Love I have known the chill of death,
From Life I have won the prize of pain.
And hope is not.

God, give me courage, send me again my pride,
Put forth Thy mighty Hand
And leave me on a bare hill-side.
Let me know the hail and the rain-storm
And the stress of warring wind.
Let me bathe my soul in silence
And forget that I have sinned.

INSPIRATION

I tried to build Perfection with my hands
And failed.
Then with my will's most strict commands.
And naught availed.
What shall he gain but some poor miser's pelf,
Who thinks for ever of his silly self?
Then to the Stars I flung my trust,
Scorning the menace of my coward dust;
Freed from my little will's control
To a good purpose marched my soul;
In nameless, shapeless God found I my rest.

Though for my solace I built God a breast.

God. thou great symmetry
Who put a biting lust in me
From whence my sorrows spring,
For all the frittered days
That I have spent in shapeless ways
Give me one perfect thing.

Anna Wickham – A Short Biography

Anna Wickham was the main pseudonym used by Edith Alice Mary Harper who was born on 7th May 1883 at 5 The Ridgeway, Wimbledon, Surrey.

Her childhood was chaotic. Her parent's marriage was disordered and her unconventional mother suddenly decided to leave for Australia with the infant Anna. It lasted a year before her Mother contracted pneumonia and Anna was placed in an institution. Her father arranged for them to return to England at some point in 1885.

Anna was encouraged to read and write from an early age but allied with this was their return, in 1890, to Australia. Her mother's teaching and character-reading career as a clairvoyant, Madame Reprah ('Harper' spelt backwards), and her father's many jobs led to an unsettled life.

In Queensland, Anna attended the local convent school followed by All Hallows' School, Brisbane (1894–6) and Sydney Girls' High School (1897–9). She seemed to not be motivated at academic life but had talent as a singer. However, her Father continued to add to her education by discussing philosophy and other subjects with her. In return Anna promised to become a poet. Her Mother meanwhile worked on grammar and elocution with her.

A return to England in 1904, initially to pursue a singing career, was partially successful. She won a drama scholarship before moving to Paris to pursue her singing in 1905.

The following year, 1906, she married a London solicitor, Patrick Hepburn and they settled in Hampstead.

The early years of her marriage were taken up with the raising of her two sons and work with the contemporary philanthropic movement, with a focus on maternal care, at St Pancras Hospital.

Her first poetry collection was published privately in 1911 under another pseudonym, John Oland. Appropriately enough it was called Songs by John Oland. The main theme of the book was the difficulties of relationships between men and women. Unfortunately, her possessive husband was very upset at her publication, having also shown little support for her earlier singing and acting careers. It led to violent quarrels and sadly Anna had a nervous breakdown and was admitted to a private psychiatric hospital for a period of six weeks.

Despite this betrayal, she later reconciled with Hepburn. (They would go on to have two more sons, Richard and George, conceived while Hepburn was on leave from war service in the Royal Naval Air Service and RAF.)

Shortly after recovering, she met Harold Monro at his Poetry Bookshop. He encouraged her writing, and this led to a second collection being published in 1915. Her life now became increasingly split between domesticity and the yearned for bohemian life that was now calling her.

During the War, whilst Hepburn was away, she struck up several literary friendships including with D. H. Lawrence and his wife Frieda. She also knew H. D., (accounts suggest they may have had an affair) and many others in the literary circle of the day.

The tragic death of her son Richard, of scarlet fever at age four, was devastating and she moved to Paris to recuperate but continued to write.

Her marriage now began to fall apart and in 1926 she separated from Hepburn although they reunited in 1928. Hepburn died the following year, 1929, in an accident on holiday. Eerily one of her earlier poems foretells the nature of his death; falling down a mountain.

During the 1930s she was well known in literary London and wrote a great deal of poetry but found it difficult to procure publication. But in 1936 John Gawsworth helped Anna to publish Thirty-Six New Poems.

In 1938 she and other feminists began a group they called the League for the Protection of the Imagination of Women.

During the Second World War her house was bombed and she lost several manuscripts and all of her correspondence.

On 30th April 1947 Anna Wickham hanged herself at the door leading into the garden at 68 Parliament Hill and, rather than a letter by way of explanation, she left a poem.

Whilst the poetry volumes she released are small in number she left behind several hundred unpublished poems that survived both the war and her life. Today she is regarded as a leading Modernist poet who was able to frankly express her desires and feelings through verse despite these often being at odds with the prevailing morals of the day.

Anna Wickham – A Concise Bibliography

Songs of John Oland (1911)
The Contemplative Quarry (1915)
The Man With A Hammer (1916)
The Little Old House 1921